CON

OR

In life sometime we get confused
Do stupid things at times
We get angry
Cheat
Sin

So we confess to self
God and Man
Say we won't do it again
Only to repeat the same mistakes over and over again

Michelle

CONFUSION OR CONFESSION

I don't know if this is the last book for 2015, but if it isn't yeah me. I know the storm is coming; I feel the calm and my dream world is truly calm.

It's silent like silent night, and I truly do not know if this is a good or bad thing. I am so used to doom and gloom; destruction, not this calm. In truth, I am truly glad for the calm because my body could not take any more doom and gloom; it needed rest and I am getting rest.

Now I don't know what to truly write now that I've finished and uploaded my book December 2015 on Lulu.com. Oh well; this is me until knowledge start to flow again.

Woke up early and can't go back to sleep, so did my little talk my way with Lovey. I asked him if we could have true justice in an unjust world? Meaning as humans; we live unjust and have unjust laws. So could we as humans live as the just if we are unjust?

When I say world I am not talking about the earth, I am talking about us as humans. The world was never created unjust, it's we as humans that make it and or her seem that way; unjust.

Ah Lovey there is so much that need to be said.

Aye sa. Wi talk bout losing friends but fren tek fren life to yass. J. Capri yu death hot to yass. Laade have mercy because shi naah mek mi live har death down. J. Jordan Joel Phillips di wurl lose yu I know, but please let me live in peace now. You are dead and gone but you are truly not forgotten; thus I DEDICATE LOSE A FRIEND TO YOU by I-Octane. I know eee hat; yu death hatta dan hot, but please truly rest in peace and leave me alone.

I cannot move on and go on with you. All I can say is truly rest in peace because the truth; the true truth of you death will be known one day. I know the full and true truth, hence your blood touched the ground; thus your vindication will come and soon. I know not what to do for you because I was warned. **WHAT DO NO CONCERN ME LEAVE IT ALONE.**

That was my warning. At times in life we do things without knowing what we are getting into. Your innocence was lost; thus you lost your life in a brutal and hot way. No one that is clean and on the road of cleanliness can go in and or walk in the realm and world of the wicked and evil. Once you do that, it is guaranteed death for you. **Yes you did not know this nor did you know that many in the dancehall fraternity belong to death. They have sold their souls; thus they promote violence; death.** I cannot change your death because what's done is done. Yes I can petition Lovey for you and in many ways my last three books talk about you. I guess this is my way of petitioning Lovey, not just for you but for true justice. Death raised their game and like I said, your death hot thus it stings.

And no Lovey, these books are not my books alone, they are yours also. I had to say my books Lovey. I did not want our readers to be confused by me saying our in sentence above. Some people may think that these books are Jordan's and mine when they are truly not.

Many of us as humans do not realize that many people say they are clean and true, but are not. I see so many things child but yet I'm powerless to make a positive difference in the lives of the few. I write, but how many read these books? You did not reach your 24th but all hope is not lost for you, so truly rest in peace. Your time came too soon but your time was right; you left earth right on time, so truly rest. Truly truly rest because in truth; I cannot linger, nor can I take death anymore. I feel it for you, but you have to rest. I know you are vindicating yourself; death, but you cannot tarry with me; you have to truly find peace and rest. Yes you are holding but I cannot go through the doors you want me to. I am not allowed; thus justice must take precedence over evil and wicked people including the wicked and evil systems men created.

Forgiveness is there, but I cannot forgive you of your sins because in truth; I know not them, and forgiveness of sins are truly not up to me. Yes you are reaching out for help; thus take the help by resting in peace. Hope is there for you because you are Capri; Capricorn and you are remembered. You will be remembered because your name and death resonate; live on in three these books.

This book and two others.

I truly do not know what else to say to you because I truly did not know you in the living nor have I met you apart from in death. Hold firm to you because if you were good and true here on earth; Lovey will truly make a way for you. He will truly not forget you.

Sacrifices are a bitch on this earth Lovey, because in order for you to make it, you have sacrifice make sacrifices unto death. Now I ask you, Why?

Why should humans; male and female including children make sacrifices unto death?

Have the children of death no stolen our riches and life? So why should anyone make sacrifices unto death in order to eat food; live?

Lovey this young ladies death does not sit right with me and I am tormented by Jordan's death. (J. Capri)

Why is her death haunting me?
I know the wrong, but why me?
Why can't I shake her death?

Is it because her death was so hot?
She needs rest Lovey so truly let her find the rest and truth she needs. I know where she went wrong but I truly did not

think it would have been her death. Yes we all make mistakes but as Bob Marley said, "is there a place for the hopeless sinner," and I did answer the question posed in this song in another book.

I did say yes, there is a place for the hopeless sinner and that place is hell. You cannot live in sin and do all that is wicked and sinful and not expect to pay for your sins. We were told, **the wages of sin is death,** *so no one should think and say otherwise. Yes some sins we can repent of them and make amends for them but we cannot wipe them off our sin record of death.* **That is why it is imperative to make sure we do good and well because the penalty of our sin and sins outweigh each good we do. Thus our sins are not just physical; they are spiritual also because we are both physical and spiritual beings.**

Ah Lovey, blood sacrifices are a bitch; thus death stings so much and it's felt by all who can see and know. And yes this is why some cry out to the living in death. Therefore, some death cling to the living for closure; true peace and rest.

Yes my body is weak; becoming weak, but I cannot let death; this death drain me. I cannot let it consume me or hold on to me. My health and welfare is at stake and I have to preserve me.

All I can ask for her Lovey is that you right the wrong that was done to her. Wow.

Thus I ask you, can justice be found in an unjust world or society?

Mi belly
Mi belly
Mi belly

Have mercy Lord because death did take its toll and it's affecting me for real.

Lovey, what does it profit a man or anyone to kill in cold blood?

Did death tell anyone to kill for him or her?

Lovey, sacrifices unto Satan and or Death is a Babylonian ritual; thing, but yet people continue with this death practice to get fame; money, power and control. Lovey did Abraham not do this bullshit and it was told in man's nasty book called the holy bible?

So tell me now Lovey, what do you want and need to do here on earth?

Right now evil cannot be contained because it's gone too far and you know this.

Why even ask me to write when you are truly not listening to me?

Why create negative forces if you Lovey knew you cannot and could not contain evil? And no, life and death in the truest of sense and world are truly not brethrens; brothers. So truly don't go there because life hath nothing to do with death. Wicked and evil people created death due to sin and gave death a home and place in their lives.

Lovey, you knew if evil got hold of life, evil would destroy all life including Mother Earth.

You knew the dangers of negative energy, but yet you let Man; Men be born with negative and evil will. Now look at the damage these men; evil and or negative forces have and has done. Earth is a testament of this negative force; energy. The universe feel it as well because the universe is plagued by negative forces; energy. Yes you've quarantined other planets so that death and or negative energy; people; humans cannot reach these planets and universes. You did good there, but earth and the universe need to be rid of evil; all facet of sin and evil. She cannot be plagued by man; wicked and evil humans anymore.

I've also told you to let evil go. So now tell me, how can we contain evil yet again so that none; absolutely no human, beast or spirit, demon or angel; release the force and forces of evil and or negative energy ever again?

Lovey, evil must die; be no more. We now know that evil cannot be contained and evil and or negative energy spread, consume and devour all that is in its path.

The body is tired now Lovey and I have to get some sleep. My energy is being drained because of her and I need to rest so that I can build up my strength yet again. <u>***So yes, I know the 24 Lovey thus 20 days before her birthday and 4 days into the month of December; thus the 13th month and 24th day. I get it; thus death is complete and had nothing to do with the 3 lions killed on Masai territory.***</u>

Death took a Capricorn; thus the sacrifices of death is complete and the dreams I had of the sacrifice that was to take place. Thus death masked death and I could not see who was truly going to die. So yes I get it, but why?

No, I should not ask you why because I know why.

I truly know why, and it's a shame one of us had to die, but as we are the beginning of life, we are also the ending; the end for all who are wicked and evil. <u>***Humans will not get it***</u> *but it's so; this is life, thus all is truly not known to man.*

So yes, Death is doing all now to piss me off but it's truly not working. In all that death do and does; Death have to die; must die; come to an end. Life; good and true life must come back to you Lovey, thus I give you good and true life clean and true.

I will not participate in death's vile and dirty games. So as there is hell; that hole and or planet that was created for death and their people; I give death their good and true home, that which is hell.

I truly lock them; Death in hell with their people and give you back the key to hell and death so that this key can be destroyed truthfully. No one can use it to open the gates of hell and destruction; chaos anymore Lovey. Create a special fire for the key to hell and death. I know what I said in another book, but hell cannot get this key lest they use it to open the gates of hell and destruction; chaos again.

Life must take precedence over death Lovey, thus the key to hell and death must be destroyed indefinitely for more than forever ever without end.

No more human sacrifices Lovey; thus I tell you to crumble these secret societies of evil and death here on earth more than infinitely and indefinitely without end more than forever ever without end. Let them rise no more but become barren and penniless globally. Let these societies find no place here on earth. All who join them and participate in the slackness and nastiness of them must become barren and penniless; void of a home here on earth and in the universe. Earth must no longer yield her blessings unto them Lovey. Neither you or Earth can continue to participate and or stay the nastiness of these vile and wicked people, people that drink urine, eat feces, drink blood and kill. Thus many say Jesus was their sacrifice unto death for man.

Absolutely no one can be a sacrifice for another human and or the next person. Sin is sin and no one can change the sins on their sin record no matter how much good they do. Those sins are recorded; thus our good and evil records that must be read back to billions of you due to death.

Lovey what do you truly need from me because I am screaming out justice to you but you are not hearing me. My world and pain mean nothing to you. Lovey someone; a female was sacrificed in Jamaica; given to the demons of hell as an offering and you are okay with this?

Why do you let death taunt me and confuse me?

I over stand her death; thus the 24 order of death and or prolific death; **THE 24 ELDERS OF SATAN; MAN.** *This death signifies something Lovey I know this, but I cannot comprehend you. When does the sacrificing of Capricorns end?*

Why the hell does death have us by the balls?
Why is death killing us?

How the hell can we talk about justice and truth when injustice prevails over good each and every day here on earth and in the universe?

Why Lovey why?

Why do good have to suffer at the hands of the wicked? Tell me because I truly do not comprehend this logic all around. Good people pay the price for the wicked; you see and know this Lovey and let it continue to happen.

Evil preserves evil at all cost you know this Lovey. Now I ask you, who's preserving the good and or good at heart; trying?

Have you not forgotten us?
Have you not left us to die?

LOVEY EVIL HAND GOOD AND TRUE PEOPLE DEATH AND YOU'RE OKAY WITH THIS!!!!

WHY SHOULD GOOD HAND OVER LIFE TO DEATH WHEN DEATH AND OR EVIL HATH NOTHING TO DO WITH GOOD; POSITIVE ENERGY?

Good and positive energy should repel all that is wicked and evil; negative, come on now. We are your children Lovey, so why are you truly not protecting us all from evil?

Don't tell me about JUSTICE Lovey when you of yourself isn't not just. You side with the unjust; thus wicked and evil people kill and get away with their wrongs come on now. You are God for crying out loud, why the hell do you permit injustice here on earth and in the universe?

Yes I know you cannot sin anyone for their truth, but for the true love of truth, do something to protect us; your good and true own.

STOP HANDING GOOD OVER TO EVIL. THIS IS WRONG AND YOU ARE INFINITELY AND INDEFINITELY WRONG TO DO THIS. COME ON NOW MAN, SAVE US FROM THE WICKED AND EVIL; EVIL FORCES THAT ROB US OF YOU.

How can I truly love evil Lovey?

I truly cannot Lovey, I truly cannot. Therefore, take back truth and secure truth with you more than forever ever without end. I will not hand life over to death; the wicked and evil. I cannot do this Lovey and you can't make me go against my good and true will. My good and true will is you Lovey and having a true good and clean; positive and pure place with you that is just and right; filled with pure love of truth.

Lovey please stop the madness because I cannot comprehend it all right now. You are suppose to be our hope and rescue; so please rescue us. I am pained by this death. It consumes my thought and now my body feels weak. So not another hour or minute must death and their wicked and evil people have here on earth. No one can live good and true in an unjust and unfair; wicked society Lovey. I can't nor can you; so why do you continue to allow Mother Earth to give wicked and evil people including children, spirits, demons and animals a home.

Why do we have to wait so long for justice Lovey?

Why do we have to lose hope because of you?

Why should we feel abandoned by you?

Why should we have to feel that you truly love evil over good; us, your children and people?

See my hurt and pain as well as the hurt and pain of others Lovey and do something. You asked me to write and I've been writing for you, but yet you see the injustice of earth and continue to hurt me so. Why?

What wrong have I done you for you to hate me so?
What wrong have I done you for you to walk away from me and abandon me so? Am I not trying for you; us?

Oh Lovey have mercy because today I am truly not the same. I am in turmoil emotionally because I cannot comprehend why wicked and evil people aren't paying for *their sins. How can a man or woman make sacrifices; human sacrifices unto their demonic gods like this Lovey?*

Dear God Lovey, where is the value in life?

Where are our morals Lovey, where are they?

Dear God how can you look at a human life and take that life from life like that?

What wrong did she do apart from sing?

Murder, this is murder; willful murder and you tell me you're okay with this Lovey?

She was a Capricorn; one of us. HER BLOOD TOUCHED GROUND AND YOU TELL ME YOU'RE OKAY WITH THIS VILE ACT!! HER BLOOD WAS ON THE ROAD; STREET. HAVE MERCY MAN COME ON NOW. LOOK INTO THE VEHICLE BECAUSE I KNOW FOR A FACT THAT THIS TRULY HAS NOTHING TO DO WITH THE HOSPITAL. AND DESPITE ME BEING TOLD BY THE DEVIL TO LEAVE THIS ALONE; I CANNOT LEAVE IT ALONE BECAUSE SHE WAS ONE OF US.

I do not belong to death nor do I abide by death. Truth and justice is life; my life and my concern and where there is injustice; like you Lovey, I have to talk about it and come to you truthfully and yes in anger with all injustice; all that is unfair and unjust come on now.

No more man, no more, no more, no more evils, no more Lovey because I truly cannot take it anymore. I am affected by sacrificial deaths. I feel the sting of these deaths come on now. My body cannot take any more of these sacrificial deaths nor can I; my spirit and true heart Lovey.

When do we as black people stop our nonsense? Hell is full of black people Lovey and instead of saving self from hell, we continue to persecute and kill our own to be in hell.

Wow because I truly don't know about us. So Lovey, truly comprehend and more than over stand where I am coming from.

Like I said, you cannot tell me about justice and have humans live in an unjust and unfair world; societies of the wicked and evil.

Injustice is not clean Lovey. It is painful and hurtful and you know this, so truly what say you?

Lovey, why do I even bother with you when you truly do not listen to me?

Why do I even bother when your ears are closed off to me?

Lovey, how can we as women be the evil ones in all of this? Why are we truly not respected?
Why do you let the wicked and evil use and abuse us?

Forgive me here Lovey but I am so going there, are you not a man in the spiritual realm? Yes, you are of both genders, but are you not male in the grand scheme of things? So why should I expect you to listen to me?

Do you not allow the mistreatment; abuse of women by men?

Are we as women not treated unfairly and ostracised by men in this world?

Are we not abused and classed as second class citizens that have no value; worth?

Did not the nasty book of man say we were the cause of sin? No, this I cannot dispute because if we had listened to you originally; these wicked and evil beasts of demonic hell holes that are called men could not hurt and abuse us; take our place with you.

Because of them many of us; not all, were locked out of your world and kingdom Lovey. Thus our ancestors faced brutality here on this earth. We were robbed and enslaved by the vile and wicked; demons of hell. Thus it's not Satan that encourage humans to sin, it's his brood; children; demons of hell.

If we had kept true to you Lovey, they; these negative and demonic beings called men could not get into our garden (vagina) and procreate with us. Yes we are at fault because we allowed them access to our good up good up and became defiled and cursed like them. **<u>Yes Lovey, I know not all men are like this because some truly respect their mother,</u>** but you have some that rule; **<u>say they rule and disrespect women, thus disrespecting you.</u>**

<u>Do these disgusting and vile things; (not all men) not know that when they rape and abuse, shame and degrade, even kill women, they are killing you Lovey?</u>

Just as not all men are wicked, not all women are clean; good. **<u>It's beyond me how we as humans say they love you Lovey and DISRESPECT; ABUSE WOMEN.</u>**

Lovey, you are both genders; so why treat males better than females?

Why keep us captive Lovey?

Women are smarter and stronger by far. WE ARE YOUR CHOSEN but yet males mistreat us and condemn us.

Can a male give birth Lovey?

Is it not females that give birth and nurture?
So why would you be against us Lovey?

No Lovey, I am not being sarcastic in anyway. Respect is due all around for everyone including you.

<u>Loyalty Lovey, thus I know the true worth of us females when it comes to you. But in knowing this Lovey, changes nothing in my book. It matters not if you favour us, we are still being disrespected and abused, raped and kill, mutilated and abandoned by men in the societies they've created to put self; men on top. Thus men put you Lovey on the same nasty and disgusting; dirty level as them.</u>

Thus men write books to prove how disgusting you are Lovey. Men depict you as the whore and murderer that procreate with human females; then turn around and slaughter your own child for the evil will of men; humans.

Men say you condone family ram business; thus their nasty and defiled, condemned book of whoredom and nastiness say you condone family ram business. Abraham and Sarah, Lot and his daughter, Adam and Eve and more.

Men put you so low that they say you require blood sacrifices to satisfy you. Abraham and his Isaac

Man even go so far and say you murdered and or allowed your son; the demon Christ and or the Christ, to be put to death amongst a murderer and a thief just to save the vile of society; this world. So tell me, what do you say in all of this Lovey?

Oh there's more Lovey, but this is not the book OUR JOURNEY/MY ANGER. I have to wane my anger; thus I am reminding you what wicked and evil men has and have done to you. They've put you as lowly and evil as them.

So now tell me, where is the truth and true justice in you?

No Lovey, I have to come to you this way. You need to think because no one can have good values and morals living in a lawless society and you know this.

NOW I TRULY ASK YOU THIS, IS THIS THE LEGACY YOU WANT AND NEED FOR SELF; YOU?

THE NASTY AND VILE IMAGES AND PICTURES OF YOU AS WRITTEN AND DEPICTED BY MEN; IS THIS WHAT YOU WANT AND NEED FOR SELF; YOUR LEGACY?

IS THIS YOUR TRUE WORTH WITH MEN LOVEY?

No think Lovey.

Is this your legacy of nastiness, murder, death, sin, deceit, injustice you; what you want humanity to continue to believe in? **<u>Are these nasty images as depicted of you by men what you truly want and need for self; you?</u>**

<u>Have you forgotten about truth and cleanliness Lovey?</u>

<u>HOW CAN YOU AS LOVEY, GOD, GOOD GOD AND ALLELUJAH LIVE WITH YOURSELF KNOWING THIS IS WHAT MEN; HUMANS THINK OF YOU AND DEPICT OF YOU? YOUR LIFE HAS NO VALUE OR WORTH TO THEM, BUT YET YOU CONTINUE TO LET HUMANS ROB YOU OF THE TRUTH; THE GOODNESS AND TRUTH OF LIFE.</u>

<u>So I ask you again, are these nasty images and pictures as written and shown in man's nasty book called the holy bible what you want and need as a legacy for self; you?</u>

The deceit stops Lovey come on now. ARE WE AS HUMANS TO TRUST MAN'S DEPICTION OF YOU?

ARE WE TO BELIEVE THEM AND THEIR LIES AND DECEIT WHEN IT COMES TO YOU LOVEY?

Well I can't believe these lying bastards, nor will I follow them because I know you and your truth.

Like I've told you time and time again, let wicked and evil people go. They have nothing to do with you, so why are you giving them a home to live Lovey?

<u>YOU CANNOT COMBINE GOOD AND EVIL; WE ALL KNOW THIS LOVEY. EVIL DESTROY AND KILL AND THIS IS WHAT EVIL AND OR NEGATIVE ENERGY; WICKED AND EVIL HUMANS AND SPIRITS ARE DOING TO THIS EARTH AND THE TRUE INHABITANTS OF THIS EARTH.</u>

Lovey, good can no longer live amongst the wicked and evil; vile beings of society globally; this earth. I've told you, Psalms One is the truest psalms in man's nasty book. So why are you not truly separating us from them; the wicked and evil? The wicked and evil are separated from the good and true of the spiritual realm infinitely and indefinitely forever ever without end. Why can't this be done here on earth come on now?

It's like when I ask you for goodness in my life you reward me with evil at times. So tell me, what the hell is the point of me or anyone that is trying to be good and clean asking you for goodness; when all you're going to do is give us evil in return?

Are you not giving us false hope and telling us that you don't give a bleep; you favour evil over us?

Are you not telling us; all you can give is evil?

Are you not telling us in your way to give up because you favour evil over us? And yes, I know you don't favour evil over us Lovey. Just truly listen to I UNDERSTAND by Smokie Norful and let him tell you how I feel at times. Thus some of the things that are written in the Michelle Jean Series of Books. This isn't about Death; Jesus Lovey. It's about you in our book and books.

Don't look at me right now Lovey, no, look at me too; see my frustration and the frustrations of others in life. So tell me, **WHAT JUSTICE DO YOU SERVE AND GIVE; IF DEATH CAN KILL YOUR GOOD UP GOOD UP CHILDREN AT WILL?**

WHAT JUSTICE DO YOU SERVE AND GIVE; IF DEATH AND THEIR NASTY CHILDREN LIVE AMONGST US AND PROCREATE WITH US; BECOME GIANTS; MEN OF RENOWN AS WRITTEN IN MAN'S NASTY BOOK; HOLY BIBLE.

Thus I've told you, Superman is flawed and weak in my book. No one that is evil should weaken truth or cast doubt upon truth come on now Lovey. Therefore, I must remind you of strength, cleanliness, goodness, honesty and truth; true justice for our good and true own; people.

No one that is wicked and evil should be allowed to come near good and clean; positive energy and people. All who are good and true; positive that are trying with you Lovey, should repel negative energy and people. We should be strong insect repellents when it comes to them.

No, don't laugh Lovey. We should repel all evil and wen dem cum wid dem blinding white light of lies and deceit, wi mirror or shield and guard automatically come up and bounce dem blinding light of evil and deceit back on them. Mek dem blind and or confused; go insane to dem ownna evil and wickedness.

No for real Lovey, come on now. I know you show us via dreams wicked and evil people. You do this to me, but before I did not know. So now I teach humanity; our good and true people about colours. Some things I know and some I truly don't, but over time you will let me more than over stand and comprehend you and what you are telling me. So no matter what evil do to me, I am still holding on to you. I just hope that you would truly listen to me and think about the circumstance (s) of our good and true people here on earth including the earth herself, the universe and good and true spirits not the evil ones, but the good and true ones that are resting in the spiritual realm.

LOVEY WAIT.

EUREKA

OH MY GOD

OH MY GOD

OH MY GOD

OMG, YU SI HOW YU LOCK OUT EVIL FROM ENTERING AND OR CROSSING OVER TO THE REALM OF THE GOOD AND TRUE MORE THAN INFINITELY AND INDEFINITELY IN THE SPIRITUAL REALM LOVEY, CAN YOU NOT DO THIS HERE ON EARTH?

CAN YOU NOT LOCK OUT ALL WHO ARE WICKED AND EVIL; ALL FACETS OF SIN AND EVIL; NEGATIVE ENERGY AND PEOPLE FROM EARTH MORE THAN INDEFINITELY NOW LOVEY?

We need this indefinite lock out Lovey. So I am asking you in goodness and in truth; true truth to lock out wicked and evil people and spirits including beasts; all that and or who are wicked and evil; truly sinful and non repentant from earth and this universe more than infinitely and indefinitely and more than forever ever without end from the earth and universe; all where evil resides? Hell is the home of all who are wicked and evil and they must truly stay in hell and burn come on now Lovey. No home or resting place must be found in earth and the universe for them. None is found in the spiritual realm for them; so no place should be or must be found here on earth and under the earth including in the universe and under the universe for them. Come on now Lovey.

Lovey, you did this for the spiritual realm, why did you not do this for earth also?

Lovey quickly lock out evil's children; all facet of sin and evil from everywhere good resides. Let this lockout be more impenetrable than that of the spiritual realm if it's possible. No, I truly don't to one up or out step the spiritual realm Lovey, but truly let the lock out of the wicked and evil, cursed and defiled, demons of wickedness of evil, evil plants and beasts, land and people be right now Lovey.

Please do not tarry come on now Lovey. We need this; all facet of sin and evil; negative energy to be locked out and gone from earth and the universe. You can do this Lovey, so do it for me and our good and true people including the good up good up good and true seeds you've given me.

Lovey, we need a new earth; a clean home here on earth. So listen to me nuh Lovey and evict wicked and evil people from earth, the universe and spiritual realm. Create that true and natural divide where good don't have to see wicked and evil people. No matter what wicked and evil people do to find us they cannot. They are blind from us; thus they go too and fro like Satan their father and find nothing.

No, Lovey, I know you can lock out all evil from this earth and give death and their people including spirits, beasts and children their walking papers.

So truly do this Lovey. I also know you can lock out evil from our lives. I know that there is a spiritual cleansing process to change; cleanse our spiritual DNA from evil and or unclean to clean so that we can reach you Lovey.

<u>So now I ask you Lovey, can this change; spiritual change and or cleansing be done here on earth too?</u>

<u>If so Lovey, let it truly be done here on earth so that we as your good and true people can be made whole?</u>

Lovey we need a clean environment for you and us and I know we can achieve this, but we need your help; I truly need your help Lovey.

So as I listen to Smokie Norful I UNDERSTAND, truly Lovey listen to me. I am in glee again.

Yes

Lovey, you have to act quickly and not delay.

Evil reached their 24000 year time limit; so turn back evil unto evil Lovey and let evil; wicked and evil people crash and burn. Lovey, you have to create life, good and true life anew and void of all that is wicked and evil; sinful and negative. Earth must become positive and positively charged once again Lovey. So let's help her in a good and true way to let go of the wickedness and evils that plague her.

Lovey please, can we, can we, can we? Can we create a new earth Lovey void of all wickedness and evil; negative energy?

Lovey can true and honest love of truth do this for me?

No wickedness and evil Lovey, please truly do not reward me with evil because the TIME OF DEATH IS UP. **EVIL TOOK THEIR FINAL LIFE AND THAT WAS THE LIFE OF A THREE LIONS AND ONE CAPRICORN.** BECAUSE OF THIS LOVEY, THE VIOLATION OF HUMAN AND ANIMAL LIFE; OUR TRUE OWN, RETURN EVIL BACK TO EVIL. THEY TRULY VIOLATED US AND BROKE THE COMMANDMENTS OF LIFE AND DEATH. SO ALL THE GOODNESS OF YOU, THIS EARTH, THE UNIVERSE, THE SPIRITUAL REALM AND ALL THE GOOD AND TRUE PLACES I'VE NOT MENTIONED, TAKE AWAY GOODNESS FROM EVIL. Let evil not find a home or place with us.

Truly let the violations and death of our own stop Lovey.

Wicked and evil people, spirits, beast, demons, ghosts, everyone who are wicked and evil must be caught up in the harvest of death Lovey. Death can no longer come for the good and take the good. Death must now take their wicked and evil own on a massive scale. Earth is not permitted to aid the wicked and evil; thus earth must run from and take away her goodness and truth from wicked and evil lands and people. These people and lands praise and worship death Lovey; so let death truly feed them and supply them with the waters and life of death; that which they need. Lovey you and I know that death cannot maintain and sustain life; thus truly good luck to billions.

And Lovey, as your daughter and protector that loves you true and more than universally and unconditionally, **<u>YOU ARE FORBIDDEN TO GIVE DEATHS CHILDREN AND PEOPLE INCLUDING SPIRITS AND BEASTS AND PLANTS WATER.</u>**

NOT ONE DROP OF YOUR WATER MUST YOU GIVE TO THEM BECAUSE DEATH'S CHILDREN ARE NOT OUR PEOPLE; THUS THEY PRAISE AND WORSHIP DEATH. THEY DESTROY AND KILL.

Lovey, if I am overstepping my boundaries with you with these words; I am truly sorry. You are my father and I cannot forbid you from doing anything, but if I could I would. So truly don't sin me or rebuke me for trying. I truly don't want or need evil; negative energy or people around us anymore.

So as I close this book, I have to talk about ROYALTY; OUR ROYAL AND TRUE HERITAGE; LIFE OF TRUTH.

I don't want to use bloodline Lovey but if I use bloodline do forgive me. ***I will use lifeline because you are our true lifeline and descent; heritage.***

Death can use bloodline and life will use lifeline.

Lovey, this morning I dreamt I was travelling. I travelled to this land; Burma. The people looked black; were black and had beautiful hair. **I saw the Jamaican Royal Flag; the Flag of Royals. The colour of the Flag of Royals is not the same colour as the physical Jamaican Flag, this flag was different and it had a Lion in the center of the flag.**

When I saw the flag of royals the Burmese officials put their flag over the Flag of Royals. Oh man I can't remember the exact wording of the question I asked. I know I asked if they (these Burmese people who looked black) were black, and was told they are Indian. I was taken to this place where they served food and for some strange reason I was helping to clean up because the place was not clean. Crabs was everywhere you would say. Some were under the wooden flooring. One particular one I got on a broom like stick and threw it away, and the small greeny blue crap bounce back to mi. Di dayam crap come latch on pon mi han. I did not want it to bite me soh mi dash eee way and *lef with dis wet white pretty sheet with this young lady. Even as I left, I did not trust the wet sheet I had because I felt crabs were in it. See sheet was folded in half long way like you would fold a sheet in the first fold if someone was folding a sheet with you.*

And for those who are wondering, the hair is not like a Somali or Ethiopian that is mixed with Babylonian (Indian). The hair and people reminded me of the people from the Dominican Republic that say they are not black and or acknowledge their blackness not. Thus they say they are white and this is truly fine by me. No place is truly found in Lovey's world for them. So yeah me and Lovey for real. Thus HELL IS FULL OF BLACK PEOPLE AND RECRUITING MORE.

I know what this dream means. Mystique you are off my travel docs and itinerary with Lovey for real. Your land I have to truly leave alone because I am forbidden to go there. Lovey don't want us to come there.

As for our royal lifeline Lovey, I am truly asking you to make our lifeline that of the spiritual realm of goodness and truth. <u>**Our lifeline can no longer be tainted by undesirables that have absolutely nothing to do with us.**</u> *You cannot let the devil continue to use* <u>**OUR ROYAL FLAG TO PROMOTE DEATH AND NASTINESS. OUR LIFELINE IS PURE AND TRUE AND IT HAS NOTHING TO DO WITH INCEST OR MARRYING FAMILY MEMBERS.**</u>

So truly stop letting these people taint our truth and world.

As ROYALS, no Lion, Lyon, Lyons can continue to taint our lifeline with you by marrying unclean men and women. We must keep clean and pure because we are of you. You have given us your name, your flag, your lifeline, genes and DNA, your truth, your goodness and peace; true peace, your cleanliness and we must now clean up self and move forward with you in goodness and in truth. We are of your line of royals and no one should come and say they are of royalty and use our flag and say they are of you when they are not. THE ROYAL FLAG IS FOR YOUR TRUE ROYALS ONLY LOVEY. No one can call themselves royal if they are not of you and you know this Lovey.

Also, as your true children, we cannot go into unclean land and lands to vacation or make a home.

We cannot conquer or colonize the wretched land and lands of evil because evil hath nothing to do with us and we hath and or have nothing to do with them; evil.

Purity of life comes through cleanliness and every good and true, pure and clean Lion, Lyon; Lyons must adhere to the truth and cleanliness of life. So I am asking you to truly evict those lying and deceitful people that are not our good and true people; lifeline from using our Crescent and name Lovey. They are not one of us and they should not use anything for us in anyway. We must protect our life with you Lovey by staying good and clean; true.

Truly reclaim the good and true Lion, Lyon and Lyons and let us continue to carry your GOOD AND TRUE NAME, CRESCENT, FLAG; ROYAL LIFELINE OF GOODNESS AND TRUTH FOREVER EVER WITHOUT END.

Lovey, no Lion, Lyon; Lyons can come and marry unclean people nor can we have unclean children ever again. You must intercede Lovey because you do with me. You must provide good and true people that are clean and honest, truly giving and truly loving for us to marry and or unify in truth with. These people cannot be from other gods of nastiness Lovey. Our good and true own are our good and true own. Thus it is unlawful and forbidden for family to marry family and procreate with family. Our lifeline to you is pure Lovey; thus you must send us and or give us good and true; clean and honest and truly loving people to lay with and or procreate with. So if good and true; clean and honest; pure and whole people reside in Russia, Africa, Ghana, Rhodesia, Kenya, Botswana, Sweden, Ukraine, Antigua, St. Vincent, St. Thomas, Netherlands, Austria, China, South Korea, Samoa and you approve of them Lovey, then let us find our way to each other and unify in cleanliness and in truth. The whoredom stops Lovey, so no, no more whoredom. One man to one woman at all times. Polygamy is a sin and it is unlawful; nasty and disrespectful on all levels, thus none of this crap in our good and true;

new society of cleanliness and truth and goodness. We made a vow Lovey, so let us keep that vow to you and self; our partner here on earth clean and safe.

So as I ask you for goodness and truth for the Lyons, Lion, Lyon, please keep us close to you. Never ever let us fail you ever again and never ever let undesirables claim and or steal our lifeline with you ever again. We are not them and we are truly peaceful people that are just.

No true Lion, Lyon, Lyons like or truly love war and strife. We frown upon unclean people including our own. We do all to stay away and not commune with negative, wicked and evil people and spirits including food and lands, waterways and trees.

Lovey you know my truth and all who read these books see this. Each good and true Lion, Lyon, Lyons stand for truth and justice and advocate for truth, cleanliness and justice come on now. Lovey, truth and cleanliness at all time. There are no underlying agenda or spirit and there should me none because I come to you with none. **<u>THE BODY AND SPIRIT MUST BE CLEAN AND REMAIN CLEAN AT ALL TIME.</u>**

So under no circumstances must you allow a Babylonian to use our Crescent. The Royal Crescent is truly not for them but for us Lovey, so truly let none defile our true lineage and lifeline. And whatever you do Lovey, truly let none latch on to me.

I refuse Babylon thus all Babylonians are refused and none can be found in our good and true world Lovey. I prepared no place for them and their nasty gods. You are my lifeline and lineage including heritage and keep; thus none must have access to me and you; our good and true people, children and lands including food, trees, waterways, language, clothing, writings, life, sex life, music, sleeping, dreams, money and true well being. You name it they are totally locked off and out more than infinitely and indefinitely without end more than forever ever without end. If they want you Lovey, let them truly find a good, clean, honest, true and pure way to you without their lies and deceit. I claim none as my own thus I truly let none in.

Lovey this reminds me of the dream I have with the Babylonian woman and man that were pretending to be with us and or one of us. Once again, with all my goodness and truth, clean and pure heart, no Babylonians allowed and if you allow one into our domain Lovey; then we will be at war truly. So as they are locked out of your realm, lock them truly out of mine. I truly do not need their lies and deceit nor do I need their stinking gods and idols of death. The devil and their children are not ours nor are they one of us. I need not have to remind you of the god and gods including idols they praise and worship; serve Lovey. Yes this is a spiritual and physical lock out Lovey. Just as how you lock out wicked and evil people and or spirits from entering the domain of the good in the spiritual world, I am asking you for the same when it comes to me; our good and true lifeline, royal crescent, children and people including the good and true seeds you've given me.

Family is truly important to me and you more than know this Lovey. So all the nastiness false pretenders; the evil ones do to discredit the true Lyons; our true royal lifeline, let them go down in flames by losing it all. No one should colonize or enslave anyone and take; rob them of their wealth and riches; life. What you've given to people and or another man or person rightfully belong to that person and or land. So in all of this Lovey, truly let justice prevail and truth reign from generation unto generation without end forevermore.

Further, let it be truly forbidden and unlawful for anyone to colonize and enslave another human being. No one and or no nation should have their right and rights brutally taken away from them by the wicked and evil; demons of this earth and universe including the demons of the spiritual realm. So truly let the latter; all that is wicked and evil pass away. Renew earth clean and true, good and honest; whole with your good and true people including me Lovey.

We truly need to build Lovey and I need you to truly build with me for the betterment of us and our good and true people. Remember my financial and health limitations in the spiritual and physical realm Lovey. Let me find true peace and hope from now on.

Let not my financial basket be so poor Lovey.

Financially I am tapped out; drained. I need to find that good Mega Mansion; Home for us Lovey. I see some but in truth, Ontario is truly not where I want and need to be. I need to find home Lovey, truly need to find home and or a good and clean home with you for the both of us.

I truly need to do and give; thus I am looking for a good and clean; true and peaceful place for me and you where we can coexist in true peace and harmony without the strife and confusion of others; manmade societies. I know all Lyons are not black in hue Lovey, some are white and a mixture of Black and White just like the good and true universe. Family, our family Lovey, must stay true to each other and we must adhere and stay clean and true to you.

Inasmuch, never forget my mother and great grandmother including grandmother. All you've sent to help me in the physical and spiritual hold everyone dear to you because they are truly dear to me. Yes Lovey, I am of Morgan, Gilfillan, which I spell Gillfillian and Gilfillian. But more importantly I am of Lyons your Royal Lifeline. Thus I have all your flags of life including your Royal Crescent. YEAH ME.

Also, I dreamt about the cross of death beneath me. You know the Pagan Cross that some European countries have on their flag Lovey. In the dream I was praying to have this cross removed from beneath me. Now I am doing the same in the living; asking you to remove the Pagan Cross of Death from beneath me as well as from around me, my family, children; those that are truly dear to me as well the good and true seeds you've given me. I see the darkness of this cross Lovey; thus I asked you in the dream to make me straight with you, thus the removal of the Pagan Cross from beneath me.

Yes one long and dark straight line was left because you did remove the head part of the cross and I truly thank you for this.

Lovey truly remember my regret of not devoting and dedicating my children to your good and true, clean and pure service. And if I can do so now that they're grown, please allow me to do so, dedicate all of them (my children) to your good and clean, positive and pure, honest and true service.

Also remember my asking Lovey; no evil must come from my bloodline which is now our good and true Lifeline Lovey. All the children my children bare; including the little one I am not sure of. If he is in fact of our good and true lifeline then truly let goodness; true goodness and cleanliness; honesty and truth come from him because I did pray good for him before he was born despite all the confusion and ugly fishes that surrounded him in the womb. Truly let my children clean up themselves and let them truly walk on your good and truth pathway Lovey. Yes I want to move out and leave them, but I must pray good and true for them because they did come from me. So every child that comes from them from generation to generation without end Lovey must be good and true, truly righteous and clean, honest and pure and void of all that is sinful; wicked and evil. None must have evil Will Lovey. Their will must be true and good all the time. They must be smart, truly peaceful and harmonious. They must be truly intelligent and wise and slow to anger. They must be physically and mentally strong; never weak Lovey. OMG, Lovey they must be truly just and kind. All must cling to you like I cling to you if not be more clingy than me. Yes that's a lot of clinging Lovey so you had better be prepared to hold hands and play.

Lovey they must do good and be good at all times. They must consider nature, this earth and universe. Oh they definitely must consider you Lovey and work with you harmoniously in goodness and in truth for the better good of all. None, absolutely none can give death and their people a home ever again. Like I've said; if death's children want a home and or place with you Lovey, let them truly find you by coming to you clean and not dirty.

When they (children from my and or our DNA and Lifeline Lovey) create and build, it must be good and true with all that is around them and with them including you Lovey.

Yes there is more Lovey and I know I should not have any regrets but I do. Oh Lovey, none that come from any true, good and true Lion, Lyon or Lyons must be stingy and greedy. Everyone must be truly giving and truly loving come on now. None can do to get. You know my loathing of doing to get and stingy; mean people.

As for me Lovey, truly let my way be straight pure with you in a good and true; positive way from now on. Never let our way be crooked.

Lovey, You are my hope and dream and I cannot lose you, so hold firm to THE ROYAL CRESCENT AND FLAG OF THE LION, LYON, LYONS AND LET NO ONE COME AND TAKE THIS; OUR TRUE LIFELINE FROM US EVER AGAIN.

<u>**I know the truth of Royals now, thus NO LION, LYON, LYONS, OR THE GOOD AND TRUE SEEDS YOU'VE GIVEN ME, MUST LAY WITH, COME AND MARRY, LIVE WITH OR AMONGST ANYONE THAT IS UNCLEAN; WICKED AND EVIL. LET IT BE FORBIDDEN LOVEY.**</u>

Truly keep unclean people from us because in truth, we do not desire them. Like I've said time and time again, you gave me seeds to plant over one hundred million acres and I need to plant those seeds good and true, honest and clean so that they grow up to you in the physical and spiritual realm, good and true, honest and clean; wholesome and pure and truly loving; caring. NOT ONE

BAD SEED MUST WE HAVE LOVEY. ALL MUST BE GOOD AND TRUE. So as we desire to be with someone in our lives, please find the right someone for us that is clean, true; pure in heart and mind, of like interest and mind as us.

So truly let people begin to adhere to the truth and clean themself up in a good and true way Lovey.

So, every last one of the seeds you've given me Lovey must be good and true; clean. Goodness begets goodness; thus cleanliness is truly you Lovey.

And Lovey, never forget; you are the final say in all of this. So truly think of you and the goodness of you. I can only write, but you are the say and stay.

Truly look at the legacy man has left you; written about you in their so called holy bible; nasty book.

<u>I will ask you again; is this the legacy you want and need for you? Is this the legacy you want humans to remember about you?</u>

You are God and no one should discredit you. If a man don't know, they truly just don't know.

Michelle

OTHER BOOKS BY MICHELLE JEAN

Blackman Redemption – The Fall of Michelle Jean
Blackman Redemption – After the Fall Apology
Blackman Redemption – World Cry – Christine Lewis
Blackman Redemption
Blackman Redemption – The Rise and Fall of Jamaica
Blackman Redemption – The War of Israel
Blackman Redemption – The Way I Speak to God
Blackman Redemption – A Little Talk With Man
Blackman Redemption – The Den of Thieves
Blackman Redemption – The Death of Jamaica
Blackman Redemption – Happy Mother's Day
Blackman Redemption – The Death of Faith
Blackman Redemption – The War of Religion
Blackman Redemption – The Death of Russia
Blackman Redemption – The Truth
Blackman Redemption – Spiritual War
Blackman Redemption – The Youths
Blackman Redemption – Black Man Where Is Your God?

The New Book of Life
The New Book of Life – A Cry For The Children
The New Book of Life – Judgement
The New Book of Life – Love Bound
The New Book of Life – Me
The New Book of Life – Life

Just One of Those Days
Book Two – Just One of Those Days
Just One of Those Days – Book Three The Way I Feel
Just One of Those Days – Book Four

The Days I Am Weak
Crazy Thoughts – My Book of Sin
Broken
Ode to Mr. Dean Fraser

A Little Little Talk
A Little Little Talk – Book Two

Prayers
My Collective
A Little Talk/A Time For Fun and Play
Simple Poems
Behind The Scars
Songs of Praise And Love

Love Bound
Love Bound – Book Two

Dedication Unto My Kids
More Talk
Saving America From A Woman's Perspective
My Collective the Other Side of Me
My Collective the Dark Side of Me
A Blessed Day
Lose To Win
My Doubtful Days – Book One

My Little Talk With God
My Little Talk With God – Book Two

A Different Mood and World – Thinking

My Nagging Day

My Nagging Day – Book Two
Friday September 13, 2013
My True Love
It Would Be You
My Day

A Little Advice – Talk
1313, 2032, 2132 – The End of Man
Tata

MICHELLE'S BOOK BLOG – BOOKS 1 – 22

My Problem Day
A Better Way
Stay – Adultery and the Weight of Sin – Cleanliness
Message

Let's Talk
Lonely Days – Foundation
A Little Talk With Jamaica – As Long As I Live
Instructions For Death
My Lonely Thoughts
My Lonely Thoughts – Book Two
My Morning Talks – Prayers With God
What A Mess
My Little Book
A Little Word With You
My First Trip of 2015
Black Mother – Mama Africa
Islamic Thought
My California Trip January 2015
My True Devotion by Michelle – Michelle Jean
My Many Questions To God

My Talk
My Talk Book Two
My Talk Book Three – The Rise of Michelle Jean
My Talk Book Four
My Talk Book Five
My Talk Book Six
My Talk Book Seven
My Talk Book Eight – My Depression
My Talk Book Nine – Death
My Talk Book Ten – Wow
My Day – Book Two
My Talk Book Eleven – What About December?
Haven Hill
What About December – Book Two
My Talk Book Twelve – Summary and or Confusion
My Talk Book Thirteen
My Talk Book Fourteen – My Talk With God
My Talk Book Fifteen – My Talk
My Thoughts – Freedom
My Heart to Heart With Lovey – God

Letters to my song and words of praise and truth; My true and unconditional Love; Lovey, Good God and Allelujah

Caged
Why
I Don't Know But I Know
Our Journey/My Anger
Real Situation
December 2015